Snow is snow, right? Wrong! there is *annui* (falling snow), *pukak* (snow that can cause avalanches), *siqoq* (swirling or drifting snow), *kanik* (rime on tree trunks)— and many other types of frosty white crystals.

This book explores the phenomenon of snow through the vocabulary of the Inuit people of Alaska, who recognize well over a dozen different types of snow or snowy conditions. In ten graphic chapters, the authors describe how a particular kind of snow is formed, its physical properties, and how it affects the lives of plants, animals, and people of the Arctic. Chapter-opening verses set the scenes, and activities and projects allow readers to demonstrate and observe for themselves.

Here is a fascinating and unique approach to the study of winter, combining scientific knowledge, the stories and myths of a far-off people, and the appeal of the familiar. Winter will never seem quite the same.

The Secret Language of
SNOW

by Terry Tempest Williams and Ted Major

ILLUSTRATIONS BY JENNIFER DEWEY

Sierra Club / Pantheon Books
San Francisco New York

For Brooke and Joan

The Sierra Club, founded in 1892 by John Muir, has devoted itself to the study and protection of the earth's scenic and ecological resources—mountains, wetlands, woodlands, wild shores and rivers, deserts and plains. The publishing program of the Sierra Club offers books to the public as a nonprofit educational service in the hope that they may enlarge the public's understanding of the Club's basic concerns. The point of view expressed in each book, however, does not necessarily represent that of the Club. The Sierra Club has some fifty chapters coast to coast, in Canada, Hawaii, and Alaska. For information about how you may participate in its programs to preserve wilderness and the quality of life, please address inquiries to Sierra Club, 530 Bush Street, San Francisco, CA 94108.

Library of Congress Cataloging in Publication Data
Williams, Terry Tempest.   The secret language of snow.
Bibliography: p. 127   Includes index.
Summary: Examines over a dozen different types of snow and snowy conditions through the vocabulary of the Inuit people of Alaska. Discusses the physical properties and formation of the snow and how it affects the plants, animals, and people of the Arctic.
1. Snow—Juvenile literature.   2. Snow—Arctic regions—Juvenile literature.   3. Eskimos—Social life and customs—Juvenile literature.
[1. Snow.   2. Arctic regions.   3. Eskimos—Alaska—Social life and customs]
I. Major, Ted.   II. Dewey, Jennifer, ill.   III. Title.
QC929.S7W53   1984   551.57′841   83-19410
ISBN 0-394-86574-X   ISBN 0-394-96574-4 (lib. bdg.)

Acknowledgments

We cannot look at winter now without reflecting on the classic work of the Russian naturalist A. N. Formozov. His research in boreal (northern) ecology laid the foundation for the important snow studies of William O. Pruitt, and we are indebted to both men.

We acknowledge Jack Major, Mardy Murie, and Peter Nabokov for their insights in reviewing the manuscript. We also appreciate the cooperation of the Teton Science School in Jackson, Wyoming, for giving us access to its library.

Jennifer Dewey's understanding of and commitment to the book gave us illustrations that beautifully express the spirit of the Far North, and Diana Landau provided keen editorial guidance and nurturing. This book belongs to all of us.

For the great pleasure derived from our work on the manuscript we thank Brooke Williams and Joan Major, our companions on skis. We are still learning from them.

Terry Tempest Williams
Ted Major

Contents

The Language of Snow

It is winter.

The Great Clouds have moved across the land,
emptying their rations of snow.
The world is new—soft and white.

The Eskimos of the Kobuk Valley
look up to the sky,
knowing each crystal
as it touches the earth and changes form.

What do we know about snow?

Is the snowflake that falls from the sky
    like the one that lands on the ground?
Are the crystals that cling to the evergreen's side
    like those that lie on its limb?
Does the season's first snow
    mix with the last?
And when the sun bursts down on white meadows
    do the crystalline flakes re-dress themselves?

Snow, as we know it, is either
powder or packed,
clean or dirty,
a little or a lot. . . .
But to the Eskimos—
snow is their special world.
Inside their minds is a name for every kind of snow
you can imagine.

To know their snow language
is to see winter
with new eyes.

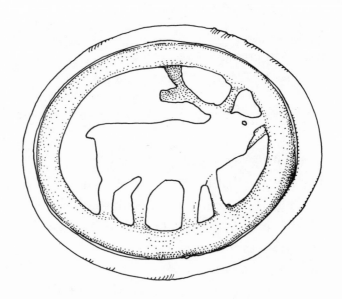

The ancient Greeks divided the world into four basic elements: earth, fire, water, and air. Perhaps they should have added one more—snow. Snow covers one-fifth of the earth's surface throughout the year. It is the most efficient system for storing water that we know of. In many parts of the world, melted snow forms a temporary reservoir for the drier summer months. In colder climates, the snow never melts completely. Instead, it forms glaciers that can last for thousands of years, a kind of permanent holding tank.

Wherever it snows a lot in the winter, the animals and plants of that place are adapted to it—that is, evolution has suited them to survive the snowy season, and in some cases they actually *need* snow to survive. Here the snow provides a warm, insulating blanket that protects animals and plants from the freezing air temperatures. We'll find out more about these plant and animal adaptations a little later on.

Snow affects the way humans live too. When the first flurries swirl around us, we sense a different feeling in the air. For some people, winter means quiet eve-

nings around the fire with hot drinks and warm conversation. Firewood is gathered and bird seed put out to help little feathered creatures through the winter; down jackets replace sweaters, skis replace skateboards. But snow sometimes means work as well as play—have you ever shoveled out your driveway?

Not many of us really have to think about living in a world that is covered with snow as far as the eye can see. However, for people in the Far North, such as the Kobuk Eskimos, snow is a way of life. In their faces you can see courage, resourcefulness, and patience— all necessary qualities for surviving the long Arctic winters. They feel the autumn wind blowing across the land and know what its cold breath brings.

Snow means something very different to the Eskimos (or Inuits, another name for Arctic peoples) than it does to us. When we look outside and see snow, we call it just that: *snow*. Most of us don't realize there are many different kinds of snow, just as there are many different kinds of flowers and trees and clouds.

The Inuits recognize various kinds of snow, and they have given each particular kind its own special word in their own language. To us, these "snow words" may sound strange, or pretty and poetic. But to the Inuit, they are full of meaning. These words tell stories.

When we see falling snow, the Kobuk people see *annui*. When we awaken to snow on the ground, the people of the Arctic awaken to *api*. They know that *pukak* means unstable snow, the kind animals dig through. *Qali* is the snow that rests in the arms of trees. They see tree trunks frosted with ice and call it *kanik*. And snow that swirls like smoke above the ridges is *siqoq*. When strong winds shape the snow into drifts, the Inuits recognize *kimoagruk*. *Upsik* is wind beaten snow, hard as the surface of a road, while *qamaniq* is the bowl-shaped hollow found around the base of a tree. And when the Kobuk walk upon *siqoqtoaq*, or sun crust, they know warm days are to follow.

All these words belong to one Inuit tribe from north-western Alaska, the people of the Kobuk Valley. Other Eskimos may use different words to say the same thing. And not only Eskimos, but people in other snowy parts of the world have their own snow language too.

A Russian naturalist named A. N. Formozov, who specializes in winter ecology, has studied the snow language of his people. Some of the Russian words are *vyuga, myatel, kurritsya, ponosukha, buran,* and *pozemka.* All these words are used to describe snow being blown around by strong winds, either in the air or along the ground.

Dr. Formozov was one of the first scientists to realize that the snow language of native peoples could be useful to science, particularly the science of ecology, which studies living things and their relationship to their environment. He found that a single word for a particular kind of snow, or snowy condition, can tell even more than a phrase of many words. For example, the Kobuk word *siqoq* gives a one-word image of a kind of blowing, swirling snow. To describe the same scene, we might have to say: "Snow that looks like smoky haze as it is blown upward by the wind." Quite a difference!

The study of snow and winter ecology is a relatively new field of science. Some biologists, like Dr. William Pruitt of Canada, have proposed a universal snow language, borrowing words from the Inuits and other people of snow to help them understand and explore winter and its effects on plants and animals. Such a universal language could be useful to scientists all over the world.

Like scientists, we too can learn much more about the wintry world by examining snow language. Perhaps if we understand the Kobuk Eskimos' words, we can begin to see snow as they do.

The People of Snow

This is not a book about Eskimos. It is a book about snow. But if we are going to try to see winter as the Inuit peoples do, through their language, we need to learn something about their way of life and why winter is such an important part of it.

Many Eskimo words will be used in this book—not only to describe snow, but also to name some things the Inuit commonly make, use, or see. The following key will help you to pronounce Inuit words correctly.

> *a:* *ah* as in "saw"
> *e:* *ey* as in "prey"
> *i:* *i* as in "stick"
> *o:* *o* as in "bone"
> *u:* *oo* as in "tool"
> *au:* *ow* as in "now"
> *ai:* *i* as in "hide"

For example, the name Inuit, using our key, would be pronounced: IN-oo-it.

The Arctic regions of the world are home to many

native tribes. This book focuses on one group of Inuit people, the Kobuk (pronounced ᴋᴏ-book).

The Kobuk Eskimos live in northeastern Alaska, in the forests of birch and spruce that grow along the Kobuk River and its tributaries. These forests are not like other forests you may have seen. They are open stretches of land with evergreen trees widely spaced. Many of the trees are dwarfed—that is, the harsh climate prevents them from growing as tall as they would in milder parts of the world. This type of forest environment is known as the taiga.

The trees of the taiga are mainly black and white spruce, aspen, poplar, and birch. Dense thickets of willow and alder border the streams, and a mosaic of plants blankets the forest floor. The deep snows of winter protect smaller plants from extreme cold and battering winds.

To the north rise the snow-topped peaks of the Brooks Range. To the south, below the Arctic Circle, the vast and treeless plains called tundra stretch for hundreds of miles. And to the west, the Kobuk River flows into the Arctic Ocean. The land of the Kobuks is defined by these natural boundaries.

The Kobuk Eskimos share the great forests with many animals, including moose, black and brown bears, beavers, porcupines, hares, and grouse. Enormous herds of caribou roam over most of the land, migrating to the mountains each summer. Dall sheep graze on steep

mountainsides, and salmon fight their way upriver to spawn.

Civilization as we know it has influenced the Inuit people of today. The building of the Alaskan pipeline has caused interest in oil drilling in the Kobuk Valley. The sound of plane and snow-machine motors has become familiar. Kobuk children go to public school, and electricity illuminates Kobuk villages. Soft drinks, candy bars, and stereos are more common in Inuit households than we might suspect. No doubt, the Kobuks' traditional way of life has changed greatly.

But some things don't change. The Kobuk people still depend on the plants and animals of the forest and rivers for many of life's necessities—and some of its luxuries, too! For example, they mix tundra greens and berries together with caribou fat to make a kind of Eskimo "ice cream," which they eat with dried fish.

As autumn approaches, people and animals alike begin preparing for the long, cold winter. Food and shelter must be provided. Just before freeze-up every year, the children of the Kobuk River Valley hunt for mousenut caches. Mousenuts are the underground stems of cottongrass, which tundra mice gather and stash away for winter fare. Large quantities of cloudberries are also collected by the Kobuk people in late August and early September. They taste a little like strawberries and are an important source of vitamin C.

Today, many of the Kobuk people live in log cabins

or houses. But it hasn't always been that way. Traditionally, an important part of the Inuits' preparation for winter has been the construction of their *ookevik*, or winter house. The *ookevik* is a turf-covered structure that is built partially underground. When we think of Inuit homes we usually think of igloos, but anthropologists now say that these sod houses were, in fact, more common.

How were the *ookeviks* built? First a site was chosen. Then the family would build a fire to soften the earth. The ground in the Arctic is permanently frozen just

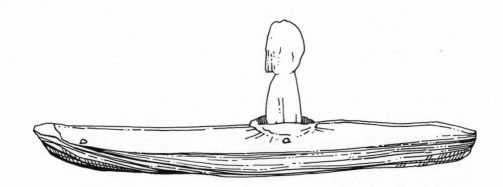

below the surface, where frozen water has been trapped underground in the soil and rocks; this is known as permafrost. The fire melted a small portion of the permafrost so that a wide hole could be dug, and the bottom of the hole served as floor and foundation. The family would continue to dig out the circumference of its home, leaving some soil piled up in the middle, where the smoke-hole would be.

Next, posts were placed to hold up the roof, and the children would gather willows to spread on the floor. The dirt that was left in the middle of the room was tossed up through the smoke-hole to cover the roof for insulation. Finally, a fire pit was constructed on a level spot in the middle of the *ookevik,* and logs were placed to mark off sleeping places, which were lined with willow down. When their *ookevik* was completed, the Kobuk River people were ready for whatever winter might bring. Some *ookeviks* can still be found in the Arctic today.

During the winter months, Kobuk men spend most of their time ice-fishing and hunting caribou, while the women work inside. Traditionally, a major project for the women has been to make fishing nets from willow bark, or *ahmaguk*. The women would take their sleds upriver until they found a suitable clump of wil-

lows. There they would cut branches about three feet long, bundle them up, and bring them home. The bundles, beautiful shades of rust and maroon, were then placed by the fire inside the *ookevik* to thaw. As they became pliable, the women peeled off the willow bark in long, graceful strips, discarding the sticks. Then the *ahmaguk* was tightly intertwined with spruce roots, making a fishing net strong enough to hold a writhing school of salmon.

Snares for trapping small animals were once made from spruce roots too, but today picture wire is used instead. This is only one example of how modern technology has changed the lives of the Kobuk people.

Now, as then, while the men and women work hard to ensure the family's survival through the winter, the children play. They may poke the earth to find little animals, or run races over the uneven, frozen ground. One game is played with a top made from a shaft of pine and a disc of spruce (or other woods, depending on what is available). The moment the top is spun, its owner runs madly out through the entrance of the house and dashes around it, trying to make a complete circle and enter again before the top has stopped spinning. Playing string games such as cat's cradle is also a favorite pastime for Inuit children. It is an old Inuit belief that string figures have magical powers: so when the dark, cold winter of the North Pole is approaching, they make a string sun to catch the real sun.

As the snow piles up outside their home, layer upon

layer, the Kobuk family spends more and more time indoors. Like other winter-bound people around the world, they entertain themselves by telling stories. Everyone listens very carefully. Listening is something the Inuits know a lot about, for they must listen in order to survive. They listen to the wind, and they listen to their dogs, who know when storms are coming. And they listen to their storytellers.

A good storyteller paints pictures with words. The stories remind you of who you are. They can make

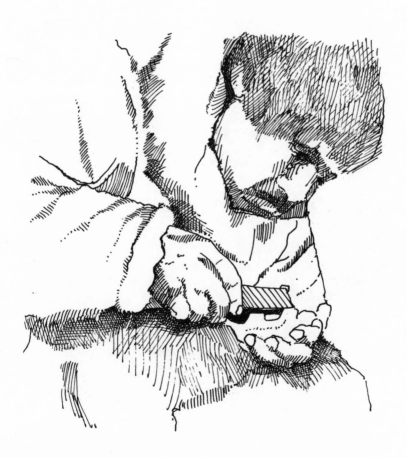

you laugh or they can scare you silly. They can even put you to sleep! Listening to a story is like watching a beautiful animal—you hate to move for fear you may miss something, and it might disappear. By sharing stories, more experienced family members such as grandparents, aunts, and uncles can pass on their knowledge and wisdom to the younger ones. The children learn how to behave; they learn about the old Inuit ways, how things used to be and what created them; and they learn about the special world they live in—all through stories.

Some of the Inuit stories are about animals who can reason and speak just like humans, and even assume human form. In these stories, just as the Inuits can remove their parkas, so the animals can remove their skins and become human.

Other stories tell about people who are helped or taught by animals. For example, in the Inuit tradition, Raven is thought to be the creator of the world; legends tell how he brought the land up out of the water and divided night from day. They called him Tulugaak.

In the Kobuk Eskimo tradition, all animals carry a story with them. It is up to each person to learn what that story is. The Kobuks say you must listen very, very carefully. Here is one traditional tale about a boy and a magical creature:

*There once was a blind boy named Tipton. He lived
with his grandmother and sister. Winter was upon them,
and they were without meat. Their bodies ached for
nourishment. One day, the grandmother spotted a blue-
black bear standing outside their home.*

"Aha!" she thought. "Now we can eat."

*They placed the bow and arrow into the boy's arms,
aiming it just so. This was a sacred weapon that Tipton's
father had made just before he died. The arrow flew
into the bear's heart, killing him instantly.*

"Did I pierce him?" cried the boy.

*Suddenly greed entered the hearts of the two women
and they thought of a way to avoid sharing the bear's
meat with the boy. "No," they murmured. "Your arrow
pierced a snowdrift instead."*

*For the rest of the winter, the grandmother and sister
dined on bear meat, succulent and juicy, while the boy
lived on a meager diet of withered berries.*

*When spring arrived, the boy took long walks down
to the lagoon. The whistling wingbeats of old-squaws
and other ducks guided his footsteps. All at once he
heard a voice that sounded like gurgling water call his
name:*

"Tipton, come! . . . Tipton, come!"

*Slowly he made his way over to the place where these
musical sounds were coming from. He felt an unusually
warm breeze. Tipton extended his hand and felt it gently
taken by another. It was Loon.*

Loon said, "Hold on to my neck, Tipton, and I will take you to the bottom of the sea."

Tipton trusted this voice and put his arms tightly around Loon's neck. Together they dove down deep, deep, deep, deep, into the cold waters. Just when Tipton thought he could hold his breath no longer, Loon brought him up to the surface and placed him on shore. Tipton opened his eyes and saw light!

Loon took him back into the clear waters again and again, four times in all, until finally his eyesight was completely restored.

Back on the shore, Tipton turned quickly to thank his healer, but no one was there. In the distance, however, he saw the silhouette of a loon. He cried with joy and praise for this wonderful act of kindness, and as his tears fell to the ground they turned into beautiful pieces of ivory. Tipton carefully gathered up each piece and made them into a necklace, strung on a strand of seaweed. He wore it home.

When Tipton saw his grandmother and sister with their swollen bellies hanging over the pile of polished

bear bones, he grew angry and hurt. The boy invited them to accompany him down to the lagoon. Because they did not look into his eyes, they did not know what was in his heart and they went willingly. As the three of them stood at the edge of the sea, Tipton quietly fastened the line of his harpoon to the women's ankles. He then arched back and hurled his harpoon gracefully into the water, and watched his grandmother and sister disappear. A few moments later, Tipton saw two white narwhals circling the bay.

"These are my relatives," he sang in a low voice. "These are my relatives."

Just then, Loon flew above him. Tipton, recognizing Loon's shadow, took off his ivory necklace and tossed it high into the air. Loon accepted the gift graciously and vowed never to take it off. And to this day, Loon is still seen wearing his white necklace of ivory.

Songs, known as *aatuutit*, are just as important to the Eskimos as stories. Like stories, they lighten the days when winter traps the Kobuk people indoors. But songs also can be very powerful and are much more than just entertainment to these people.

Orpingalik, a Netsilik Eskimo, says that songs are "thoughts which are sung out with the breath when people let themselves be moved by a great force, and ordinary speech no longer suffices." When Inuits are gripped by a powerful emotion, they do not struggle against it, for they believe that such feelings come from

a great power outside of themselves, and they become a part of that power. Orpingalik says, "A person is moved like an ice-floe which drifts with the current. His thoughts are driven by a flowing force when he feels joy, when he feels fear, when he feels sorrow. . . ."

There once was a woman, Uvavnuk, who on a dark, clear night received her sacred gift of inspiration. She was looking up at the sky, when all at once a meteor came rushing out of space and found its home inside her. She was filled with more and more light, until she who had always been a woman of silence was trans-

formed into a holy person who could sing songs th
radiated the warmth and brilliance of a glowing mete

Songs traditionally are used to bring success in hu
ing and to control the weather. An old woman tells of
a time when she was a young girl and had gone out
with a friend to pick berries. A wind came up and
encircled them. It began to snow. The girls became
very frightened and were unable to make their way
home in the blizzard. Suddenly, as if by a miracle,
the clouds cleared and they found their way home in
safety. There they discovered that a relative had been
singing a weather song for their benefit. By changing
the direction of the storm, she had saved them.

And so, with work and play, stories and songs, the
long winter passes, and the Kobuk people welcome the
coming of spring. But they know the winter snows will
always return. Though many things in their lives have
changed, the Arctic winter is much the same for them
as it was for their ancestors. The snow shapes their
lives, and they adapt to its presence in ways both old
and new.

Let's go outside now, into our own world of winter,
and find out how the Kobuk peoples' snow language
can tell us stories, too.

THREE

ANNUI
Falling Snow

Annui:
Feathers are flying everywhere.
Someone has broken the cloud pillows open.
Snow is falling and
Earth's face is changing.
Flakes upon flakes fall
on the wrinkled landscape.
Autumn's colors are quieted—
red-yellow to brown, now white.
Listen—
silence is settling in.

The first snowfall of winter is an exciting event. Billowy gray clouds release huge quantities of what looks like white confetti. Each bit of confetti, each snowflake, having just completed an incredible journey through the atmosphere, lands quietly. Sometimes it lands on us.

Have you ever tilted your head way back and watched snowflakes drift to earth? If so, you may have felt the soft flakes tickling your face, or piling up on your eyelashes. Have you ever tried to catch snowflakes with your tongue as they fall? Or to keep one snowflake by itself in your hand?

Falling snow, when seen through Kobuk Eskimo eyes, is called *annui.* Where does it come from? How is it made?

Annui, or falling snow, occurs when water vapor in the atmosphere gets cold enough to form clouds. This usually happens when the air temperature is near freezing, somewhere in the range of 32° to 39° Fahrenheit, or 0° to 4° Centigrade. Clouds are actually clumps of very tiny ice particles. When conditions in the atmosphere are just right, these ice particles grow larger, with the addition of either condensed water vapor or microscopic flecks of salt or dust that have been blown upward by winds. The particles grow until they become so heavy that they fall to the ground as snow.

When the particles leave their cloud, they are in the form of tiny six-sided ice crystals. In its simplest form, snow is an assortment of many different crystals. The shape of each crystal is determined by the temperature and humidity of the air in which it is formed. That's the reason no two snow crystals are exactly the same.

The journey of the snow crystals takes them down and down, through layers of cool air and layers of not-so-cool air, through layers of wet air and layers of dry air. All of these differences help to create the tremendous diversity among snow crystals.

As the snow crystals, now in millions of different shapes, are about to land on the earth, the temperature of the air also determines *how* they will fall. For example, when the air near the ground is cold, snow crystals fall separately. But when the air near the ground is warmer, snow crystals melt together to form large clusters of wet, sticky snow. We sometimes call the separate crystals snow "flakes," but technically speaking, snowflakes are *clusters* of crystals.

With snow crystals falling in so many different shapes and designs, how can we study them all? Scientists have classified falling snow into as many as eighty different categories. But we will use a simpler system, one proposed in 1951 by the International Commission on Snow and Ice. This system groups snow crystals into seven basic structural types: stellar crystals, plate crystals, spatial dendrites, irregular crystals, needles, columns, and capped columns. Almost all snow crystals will fit into one of these seven categories. Let's learn how to recognize them and how they are formed:

Stellar Crystals   Stellar crystals look like snow "stars"—the beautiful crystals we all think of when the snow flies. They hold delicate patterns within their six-pointed framework, which radiate from the center like the spokes of a wheel. Stellar crystals form inside low clouds, where warm temperatures and moisture are present. Because of their starlike points, individual crystals readily connect, then descend as larger snowflakes. These snow stars, looking like miniature two-dimensional doilies, drift downward very slowly, very gently, creating a peaceful mood.

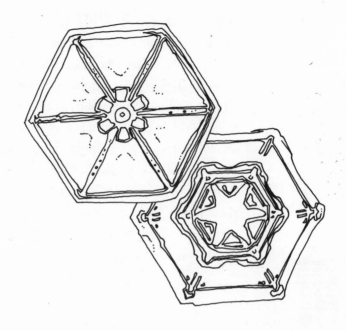

If you are fortunate enough to catch a plate crystal, **Plate Crystals**
you will quickly see that it is a perfect hexagon. Six
smooth sides frame a flowerlike pattern within. Plate
crystals lack the points of the stellar crystals that make
it so easy to link up one with another, so a plate crystal's
journey to earth is a solo performance. But plate crystals
perform beautifully on their own: when light conditions are favorable, they act like prisms, refracting color
in a seemingly colorless world. Stellar crystals and plate
crystals frequently coexist in the same snowfall.

Spatial Dendrites If stellar crystals look like miniature two-dimensional doilies, spatial dendrites look like little three-dimensional ones. That's because they have additional projections sticking up at right angles from the flat surface. The branches or arms of these snow stars are connected to each other every which way, instead of in an orderly six-sided design on a single plane. Spatial dendrites are born as stellar crystals, but while they journey to earth through different atmospheric conditions they change their form. Colder temperatures cause deposits of frozen water droplets to cling to the original stellar crystal, turning it into a spatial dendrite.

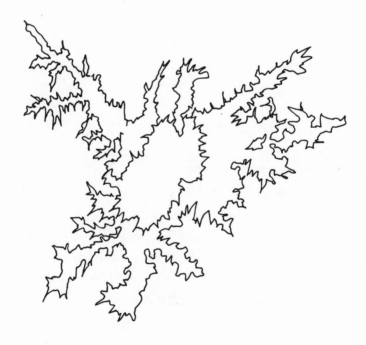

This is a large category of platelike crystals joined to- **Irregular Crystals**
gether in odd, free formations. Like stellar and plate
crystals, they are born in low, warm, wet clouds, but
they change form as they drift down to earth. With a
little imagination you might see these snowflakes falling in the shapes of white kittens, rabbits, butterflies,
or maybe even letters of the alphabet!

Most snowstorms drop needle crystals—long, slender **Needle Crystals**
six-sided columns with sharp points at either end. Like
stellar crystals, they stick to one another, freeze together, and form large snowflakes. Needle crystals drift

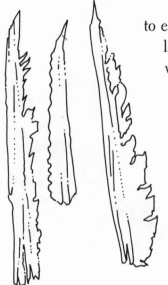

to earth slowly, but when they land on a hard surface they will shatter into many fragments, resembling tiny splinters of ice.

Column Crystals Column crystals are tiny six-sided tubes of ice with either flat or pointed ends. They're often hollow and contain an air space inside. They are formed within cold, dry, and very high clouds that look much like pulled swabs of cotton. These cirrus clouds are made up almost entirely of column crystals. When clouds containing these crystals pass in front of a full moon, an elegant, rainbow-colored halo is created.

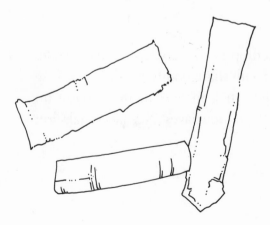

A capped column is an example of a combination crystal. In this case, it is a column crystal with a hexagonal plate at either end. Capped columns are formed when ice crystals travel through cold, dry atmospheric conditions, where they become column crystals, and then continue to fall through a warm, wet layer of air that produces plate crystals.

Capped columns have also been called *tsuzumi* crystals because they resemble the Japanese *tsuzumi* drum.

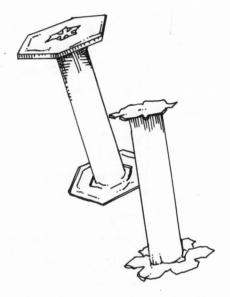

The International Snow Classification system also includes a few kinds of frozen precipitation that are *not* actually snow: graupel, hail, and sleet, or ice pellets. Graupel and hail are formed by the same basic process. They begin as ice crystals, falling through a cloud or misty layer of super-cooled water droplets. These droplets can remain liquid even at subfreezing temperatures as long as they are suspended in air, but as soon as they touch any solid object—such as a snow crystal—they freeze into an icy covering called rime. So graupel and its relatives are known as heavily rimed crystals. Sleet is somewhat different. Let's explore all three in more detail:

Graupel *Graupel* is the German word for soft hail. Perhaps you have felt small pellets stinging your face during an intense snowstorm, or seen them lying on the surface of the snow. Chances are you were experiencing a graupel shower. Graupel begins as stellar or plate crystals. As they fall through the atmosphere, they are buffeted by the wind and coated with ice droplets—the coating we call rime and the Kobuk Eskimos call *kanik*. Usually graupel falls for only a few minutes during longer snowstorms. When it hits the ground, it bounces off hard objects and surfaces. Sometimes graupel can create avalanche conditions because it forms an unstable base, and snow layers on top of it can slide off.

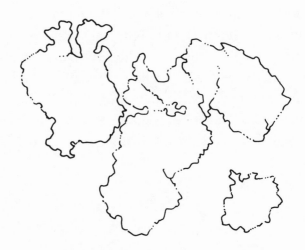

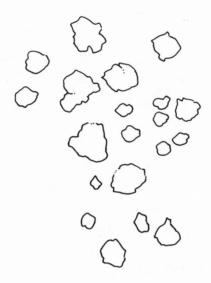

Hail is formed in basically the same way as graupel, but in warmer temperatures. Droplets of moisture falling to earth are caught in updrafts—currents of air that toss them back up into the atmosphere. Each revolution adds another coat of ice, until the hailstone becomes so heavy that gravity pulls it to earth.

Hail

Sleet begins as rain but as the water droplets descend through cold layers of air near the ground, they freeze, becoming small ice pellets. In the middle of a rainstorm in cold weather, you may notice the rain growing "thick" and the ground slushy. This is probably sleet.

Sleet, or Ice Pellets

It is important to remember that each type of snow crystal is formed under different environmental conditions. The kind of crystal that falls to earth as *annui* has a great effect on the kind of snow cover we will find later. Snow can possess many different qualities and personalities, depending on how much water, ice, and air it contains. Snow with a high water content acts like plastic. This kind of snow, which contains mostly stellar and plate crystals, can be molded into perfect snowballs and even squeaks with the pressure from your cupped hands. Another type of snow, commonly called powder snow, contains mostly capped and column crystals. This snow is so loose and fluffy and dry that it's practically impossible to pack.

Temperature and wind conditions near the ground also affect what happens to *annui* after it falls. It can form a soft, fluffy layer of snow, providing a playground for skiers, or it can harden into an icy surface that can serve as a winter highway for both animals and humans in the Arctic. It can produce a heavy, wet blanket that may cause spring avalanches, or form a loose, yielding layer of snow. This last kind has insulating properties that help tiny burrowing animals, such as mice and shrews, as well as many insects and plants, to survive in regions of long, harsh winters.

Annui has fallen everywhere from San Francisco to Miami Beach, but the high mountains of the American West capture by far the greatest amounts. A record seventy-two inches has been known to fall over a twenty-four-hour period in the Colorado Rockies!

Snow is a white serpent with many heads. It can disrupt a city the size of New York, repel invading armies, or protect animals from the sting of freezing temperatures. It can store our water or immobilize our highways. A snowstorm can be a gentle shower of feathery flakes or a blinding, suffocating, wind-driven blizzard. Each year the first snowfall of the season is greeted with both celebration and apprehension. It is as though we have just seen it for the first time in our lives. *Annui!*

A CLOSER LOOK AT *ANNUI*

To examine the various snow crystals more carefully, take a piece of black construction paper and put it in the freezer at least overnight. During the next snowfall, take your paper outside and let the crystals land on its surface. Because the black sheet is cold the crystals will last longer, thus enabling you to identify just what kind they really are. A hand lens or magnifying glass can aid you in your classification. Stay outside for a while; you may find one type of snow crystal falling, then suddenly another type will appear and mix in before taking over. This tells you that remarkable changes are taking place far above you! But be careful: the sun's warmth or your moist breath can quickly melt the beauty of these incredible snow flowers!

API
Snow on the Ground

Api:
A quilt has been made
by a circle of clouds
and draped
across the land.
Shrew, Deer Mouse,
Weasel, and Vole
move beneath
its cover.
Snowshoe Hare leaps gracefully
over deep snow;
Lynx may be nearby.
Grizzly and Ground Squirrel
are sleeping—
their heartbeats are slow
and hidden.

After its journey through the sky, *annui*, or falling snow, finds its way to another personality as it settles on the ground. *Annui* becomes *api*.

Not only do snow crystals change as they fall through the atmosphere, but they continue to change and alter their structure long after they reach the earth.

This process of change is called snow metamorphism. Just as a caterpillar is transformed into a butterfly, so *annui* is transformed into *api*. The process starts right away and never stops. As soon as it reaches the ground, the snow crystal's fine detailed structures begin to disappear. The delicate outer parts of the crystal evaporate and condense until its center becomes a small granule of ice. This undressing and redressing of the snow crystal is also called age hardening.

Perhaps the easiest way to understand how it all works is to stop thinking about snow as separate ice crystals falling to earth. Instead, picture *api*—snow on the ground. Picture vast areas of snow like a blanket over the land, and picture it in layers, like several blankets piled up: the first snowfall, covered by the second snowfall—perhaps melted by the sun and shifted by the wind—then a third snowfall on top. Now we're ready to understand the changes going on inside all those layers of snow.

There are three main processes involved. The first process is called *temperature gradient metamorphism* (by this we mean that the snow is not all the same temperature). When the bottom layers of snow are much warmer than the top layers, water vapor rises from the lowest layers and is deposited on the cold upper layers. The result is a bottom or an in-between layer of enlarged snow crystals with flat, steplike sur-

faces and angular corners. They look much like sugar crystals.

Such snow is called depth hoar by us, and *pukak* by the Kobuk people. Like sugar, it is loose and granular. Small animals such as mice, voles, and shrews need a loose, yielding snow that will shift and move with their body weight. They can tunnel through these delicate crystals without much trouble and build their winter nests. Moose, elk, deer, and caribou—animals that paw with their front feet to uncover plants buried beneath the snow—also seek this same loose, yielding snow.

Pukak helps insulate plants and animals from the cold because the temperature between the first layer of snow and the earth usually remains close to 32°F., or 0°C. This "winter heat" is supplied by the unfrozen soil below and by air pockets within the *pukak*.

The second age-hardening process is referred to as *equitemperature metamorphism*. It occurs when the temperature is about the same throughout the snow pack. New crystals lose their tiny projections and form rounded particles of ice. These bond together tightly to form a dense, stable snow mass. Equitemperature snow is shunned by both small and large animals. A caribou or deer that spends all its energy digging in firmly packed snow is lessening its chances for survival. The same principle holds true for the smaller animals: trying to burrow into hard, compacted snow is just too much work!

The third process of age-hardening is called *firnification*, or melt–freeze metamorphism. It takes place when the snow melts and then freezes, sometimes several times. When the snow absorbs the sun's rays, melting occurs, and the crystals lose their delicate points. But when night comes and temperatures drop, the remaining central parts of several crystals freeze together and become one large crystal. These large poly-

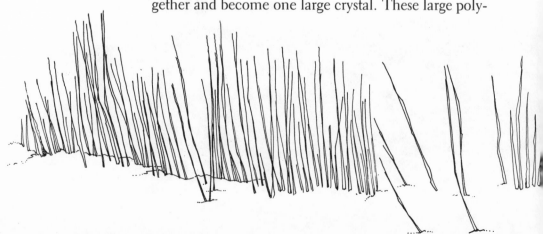

granular crystals then freeze to each other, forming a very solid layer of snow.

The strength of the snow pack will vary, depending on whether the layer is in the melt or the freeze stage of the cycle. Can you remember walking on top of the snow in the morning, but sinking deeply into your tracks later that afternoon? The faint footprints you made during the colder hours become puddles of slush as the temperature rises. The next morning, after the cycle is repeated, you can see the frozen imprints of the previous day's journey. This illustrates the firnification process.

This type of metamorphism can produce what scientists call *nast*, a Russian word for an icy crust. Some animals can travel on this surface, while others not as well adapted will break through and flounder, becoming easy prey for predators.

Animals and *Api*

For many species of animals, *api*—snow on the ground—is the most important limiting factor in their relationship with winter. Their survival depends upon how well they can adapt to the snow. How well or how poorly they are adapted to different snow covers directly affects their ability to move, to obtain food, and to avoid *becoming* food! Coping with winter consumes a

tremendous amount of an animal's energy, and unusually severe conditions can almost wipe out an entire population in a given area. The depth, density, and hardness of the snow can help or hinder animals, depending on the situation. For example, icy crust can be disastrous to a tiny shrew trying to burrow into the snow to escape the talons of the great gray owl. But the wolf, who depends on an icy crust to support his weight as he chases a caribou, may lose his prey if the snow cover softens.

Animals survive winter through various kinds of adaptations. Some animals undergo physical changes. The claws of a particular lemming, for example, grow longer in the winter for digging in snow and are shed in the spring when they're no longer needed. These are called deciduous claws, like deciduous trees, which lose their leaves in the fall. The weasel's brown coat of summer becomes white in winter. (It also gets a name change: weasel becomes ermine!) Some small animals change their behavior. For instance, shrews and voles disappear under the snow to seek insulation from the

cold. Other animals either hibernate (ground squirrels) or migrate (caribou).

The Russian naturalist A. N. Formozov has grouped animals into three different categories according to their ability to adapt to snow—in other words, their "snow tolerance."

Animals that possess special adaptations related to snow—such as the ability to turn white or grow thicker fur or special winter feet—are classified as "snow lovers," or *chionophiles* (Formozov used the Greek word *chion*, for "snow," as the root for his classification system). The musk ox, polar bear, caribou, snowshoe hare, lemming, lynx, Arctic fox, snowy owl, and ptarmigan are all members of this group.

Musk oxen, which came into existence during the Ice Age with mammoths and woolly rhinoceruses, have developed a protective covering of insulating hairs. These coats of Arctic armor are the key to their survival. A fine wool covers their skin much like a woven blanket. This cover is called *quivit*. It is extremely thick and matted, and serves as an airtight capsule. Over this soft layer of fur lies a coat of long, brown guard hairs. The two coats trap a warm layer of air between them, protecting the ox even in a paralyzing storm.

Musk oxen do not migrate from the tundra during the winter and are the only animals that can weather

a blizzard simply by standing still. Their broad, rectangular bodies, short legs, and shaggy fur make them just about weatherproof. They wait the storm out quietly and patiently—sometimes for days. Their lives are in danger only if deep drifts begin to form or if wolves are about. When this happens, these enormous animals band together and form a protective huddle, with the young pushed into the center and the able-bodied males standing guard on the outside. The warmth of the herd and the defensive pose of the older bulls help ensure the survival of all.

The musk oxen's ability to wait out storms for days at a time is helped by their tendency to gorge themselves with food during the short summer season. That gorging builds up their bodies' fat reserves, so when food becomes scarce they can live off their stored fat for weeks at a time.

Caribou are almost as well adapted to Arctic winters as musk oxen. But one major difference between them is the caribou's vast migrations. Thousands of caribou travel every year from their summer feeding grounds on the tundra to the forested taiga where they spend the winter. This trek is largely motivated by a search for food supplies, especially a small plant called reindeer lichen.

Caribou abandon the tundra and its hard-packed snow cover in late autumn and move into the forested taiga, selecting high routes where the snow depths are shallow. Here they can paw easily for reindeer lichen,

which they can sniff out even under a foot of snow. Caribou can tolerate a depth of snow up to two feet, depending on how dense and hard it is. To avoid deeper snows they also travel on wind-hardened drifts.

Physical adaptations as well as migration help the caribou survive winter. Each hair in the caribou's coat has a tubular center filled with air, which greatly increases the coat's insulation value. Kobuk Eskimos traditionally have prized caribou skins above all others. They made their parkas from caribou hides, and extremely waterproof boots from the skins of caribou legs.

As the caribou move across the tundra in their long,

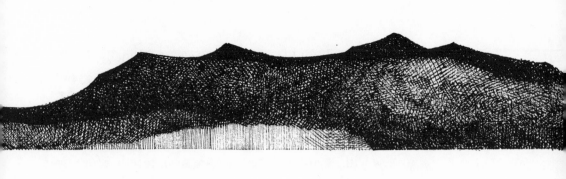

strenuous migrations, a distinct clicking sound can be heard. It's their ankle joints! Caribou ankles are more flexible than those of any other member of the deer family. This flexibility helps them walk across the spongy and uneven surfaces of the Arctic tundra. Also, caribou hooves fan out when the animals walk on tundra, much like a human hand with its fingers spread. This gives the caribou a broader base for balance on snow or ice. And the hooves have a sharp outer edge, helpful when they are pawing for food in crusty snow, or need extra traction on ice.

Tuttu, as the Kobuk people call caribou, are important to Inuit life in many ways. Traditionally, Inuits have depended on caribou not only for clothing, but for food, tools, and fuel. When a caribou is killed, very little of the animal remains unused. Bones are sharpened into tools, such as awls for the women to sew with. Caribou intestines are sewn together for rain gear. Oils from the animal's fat are burned as fuel. And, of course, caribou meat provides food for them. The Inuits therefore follow the caribou migration from one point to the next. Where the caribou settle, the people settle and prepare themselves for the hunt.

Because caribou are so essential to the Inuits, the hunt becomes a special, sacred act. Great care is taken not to offend the caribou. Throughout the winter, Inuits perform rituals and sing songs, all meant to induce the caribou to come to the Inuits. And why would the caribou do that? Because, according to Inuit legend,

animals treated with respect allow themselves to be taken. Mystery surrounds this ancient bonding between Inuit and caribou.

Animals such as the moose, wolf, and wolverine, which are still in the evolutionary process of adapting to snow, are grouped by Professor Formozov under the name *chioneuphores*. The moose's anatomy is very well adapted to snow. A moose looks as though its body has been placed on stilts. Its long legs reach down through the snow to the firm ground below, carrying its belly well above the surface. Each leg is lifted with an angular motion, swinging up, out, and around with grace and precision. In contrast, elk and deer have to plow their way through deep snow with their chests, using up much more energy. Their tracks tell the story: a moose leaves a "clean" track in the snow, whereas an elk makes a trough.

Formozov's third category of animal adaptation to snow consists of creatures that are *not* adapted to it, and actually avoid it. They are termed *chionophobes*. Pigs, opossums, domestic cats, and many small birds fall into this category. Naturally, such animals are not found in the Arctic.

Winter Sleepers and Heat Savers

What about animals that hibernate? Hibernation is a deep winter sleep. It's common to many groups of animals, including insects, snails, amphibians, reptiles, and mammals.

There are no amphibians or reptiles in the Arctic, simply because it's too cold. Most of these creatures bury themselves in soil or mud to hibernate, but Arctic soils are frozen just a few inches below the surface (permafrost). In many other parts of the world, however, frogs hibernate by burying themselves in the leaves and mud at the bottom of ponds. Toads back into the ground, digging well below the frost line with their horny heels.

Rattlesnakes often seek winter shelter in a mountain cave. So do bats, who spend winter months in closely packed groups, looking like giant balls of fur. Some butterflies pass the winter in hollow logs, taking flight once again when temperatures rise.

True hibernating mammals include jumping mice, ground squirrels, prairie dogs, northern bats, marmots, and badgers. Bears are famous for hibernating, but their winter sleep is not true hibernation. It is a period of dormancy—what biologists call a torpid state—where the bear's body functions slow down greatly to conserve

energy, but the bear could still awaken if disturbed. Raccoons, skunks, and chipmunks do the same.

True hibernation is still a mystery. We do understand some of what happens to an animal when it is in this deep winter sleep. Body temperatures drop to match its surroundings, usually a few degrees above freezing.Breathing slows way down. For example, the ground squirrel, who takes 187 breaths per minute in July, breathes only 1 to 4 times per minute in January. Blood circulation is also reduced, with heartbeats decreasing as much as thirty percent in winter. We do not understand, however, the many chemical changes that occur within the animal during hibernation.

The length of a particular hibernation period depends on many factors: the kind of animal, its food supply, location, weather, and light conditions, and of course, the temperature. Scientists are interested in hibernation for many reasons—one is the hope that someday astronauts might be sent into space in a hibernating state to conserve energy so they can stay out longer!

Arctic animals that don't hibernate spend much of their time trying to stay warm. One of the most serious problems for animals in winter is heat loss. Anything that reduces an animal's "heating" needs increases its chance of survival. Even size counts. Animals with short extremities, such as short ears and legs, save energy. But the larger the animal overall, the smaller its surface area in relation to volume, and as a result, the less heat it will lose. In the Arctic, both laws apply: musk oxen do have short legs and ears, and moose grow much larger in Alaska than they do in Wyoming.

Other heat-saving devices look obvious. Large mammals grow a thicker coat of fur for winter, and put on more body fat, which serves as insulation. But no animal, large or small, can cover all of its body with insulating fur. Footpads, hooves, and noses must be left uncovered if they are to function properly. Knowing how cold your own nose can get on a bitter day, you might well wonder why an animal's nose doesn't freeze.

The explanation is simple. Nature has evolved a very effective process: the warm outgoing blood in the arteries heats the cool blood returning from the extremities, such as the feet. This exchange occurs in what

biologists call a wonder net—a network of small arteries and veins located between the main part of the animal's body and the extremities. As a result, a wolf's paws can become much colder than the rest of its body without losing their ability to function or draining off internal heat. This net also allows the animal to release excess heat from its body. Otherwise, a heavily insulated animal with thick fur would soon become overheated. The same principle applies to ducks and other birds that stand on ice, and to seals, dolphins, whales, and walruses, who swim in chilly waters.

Many types of animal behavior are designed to reduce heat loss. Birds fluff their feathers, enlarging the "dead air" space around their bodies. Quails roost in compact circles, in the same manner as musk oxen, to keep warmth in and cold out. Grouse and ptarmigan dive into the snow, using it as an insulating blanket.

Animals that store food are using another behavioral adaptation. Winter offers advantages to seed-eating creatures. In autumn, many weeds, bushes, and trees produce abundant seed crops. These are high-energy foods, conveniently packaged. Dry foods of this kind are stored by pikas, beavers, deer mice, and squirrels. Clark's nutcracker, a hardy bird of winter, buries nuts,

seeds, and berries in many caches—sometimes more
than a thousand! They have been known to retrieve
seed stalks from a Douglas fir cone eight inches below
the snow!

Api tells many stories: of changing crystals, of aging
snow, and of animal survival. What at first appears to
be a bare and quiet snow cover, we now know is the
stage for many acts of Arctic drama.

TRACKS TELL THE TALE

The next time you find yourself walking through the snow in the country, keep your eyes open for the signs animals leave behind. If you look closely you may see hundreds of footprints and wingprints, each with its own story to tell.

What about the tiny tracks that run in circles and disappear where wings have fanned the snow? Perhaps a meadow vole fell prey to a rough-legged hawk. Then there is the weasel (or ermine in winter), who leaps and bounds across the snowfield until its tracks abruptly stop—only to reappear some distance ahead. This tells us that ermine can "swim" through snow (they seem to do this for pleasure as well as for prey!). Watch for the snowshoe hare, whose large back feet "leapfrog" over its front paws, making two wide tracks and two narrow ones, two wide and two narrow . . . all the way to the base of a big spruce tree, where he can hide under protective boughs. Each creature leaves its signature in tracks and tails, feathers and fur.

FIVE

PUKAK
Snow That Can Cause Avalanches

Pukak:
Winter's drama.
Temperatures coax
a costume change,
as crystals wear masks
of opposing characters.
Act One:
sugar snow—
sweet and supple,
perfect for small creatures
to tunnel in.
Act Two:
depth hoar—
hanging on steep slopes
where ball bearings roll,
loosing waves of snow.
Listen
for a crack in the night:
the rumble and roar
of Avalanche!

It is early winter, about the time the Eskimos of northern Alaska expect to see Kukuweaq, the ten-legged polar bear. They are told at a very young age: "If you see five men standing together, and it looks like they are wearing sheepskin parkas, don't go to them! That is the polar bear with ten legs."

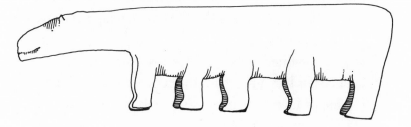

The snow has spread a thin white sheet across the landscape. Beneath this cover, the soil is many degrees warmer than the air. When this happens, we say that the temperature gradient is very high. This difference in temperature makes the whole sheet of snow change. Near the ground, water molecules evaporate from the tips of the warm, partially melted snow crystals and flow upward, attaching themselves to the larger crystals in the upper, colder layers of snow. The lower layers—usually part of the season's first storm—take on an angular, loose, granular structure. Gradually the ice crystals next to the ground may erode away completely. They leave behind spaces like small tunnels, decorated with fragile latticelike walls and ceiling of snow under the thicker snow roof. This loose, delicate snow, which looks much like sugar up close, is called *pukak* by the Inuits. As we mentioned in Chapter 4, it is also known as depth hoar, and backcountry skiers call it TG (temperature gradient) snow.

Pukak is very important for small mammals. Because it is loose rather than solid, shrews, voles, mice, and lemmings can tunnel through it. Try to imagine what it must be like for a vole as he scurries through the icy darkness of *pukak*, rearranging the loose sugar crystals with his elongated winter claws, searching for food and a cozy grass-lined nest. Perhaps his tunneling makes these crystals hiss and groan, the eerie echoes bouncing off stronger layers of snow as the vole moves through his underground world.

Pukak also acts as an insulating blanket, holding in warmth that protects tiny creatures. Without it, they would surely have a difficult time surviving the harsh Arctic winters. Several feet of *pukak* is generally enough to keep temperatures almost constant, day or night. In fact, *pukak* actually stabilizes the temperature in the space between earth and snow, usually close to the freezing point (32°F. or 0° C.). It is remarkable how

good an insulator snow is. Ground and air temperatures can differ by as many as ninety degrees. When the Arctic wind roars across the tundra and temperatures drop to a −60°F. (−51°C.) or lower, the vole may be enjoying a comfortable 30°F. (−1°C.) several feet below the surface!

Think about it: How can something cold and wet like snow keep a creature warm? The answer lies in the amount of air trapped within the snow's crystal framework. Between and around each snow crystal is air. The more "dead air" (it can't escape) inside snow, the greater its insulation value. Look at the little chickadees and white-crowned sparrows, who don't migrate south when winter comes. When it gets cold they puff up their feathers until they look twice their normal size. What they are doing is adding air space around their bodies to keep warm. The Inuits also know how to do this. They dress in layers, and between each layer of clothing

is another layer of trapped air. Because *pukak* is loose and granular, a great deal of air gets trapped inside. This is one of the reasons why snow can keep animals and plants warm.

Many animals take advantage of *pukak*. The caribou paws through this soft layer of snow in search of lichen and other tundra vegetation. Dall sheep also get at their food this way. The willow ptarmigan, a member of the grouse family, is equipped with special digging combs on its feet, which it uses to brush away the top layers of snow until the sugary *pukak* is uncovered. When they roost at night, the birds cover themselves with these loose crystals; it's like putting on a protective cloak. In the Rocky Mountains other members of the grouse family do the same thing. You can see evidence of this behavior in their foot tracks and wingprints in the snow.

But although *pukak* is a tremendous aid in animal survival, it sometimes causes trouble when it accu-

mulates on steep slopes. The loose, granular snow can become very unstable, acting much like a layer of ball bearings on top of a metal sheet. If the snow layers above the *pukak* become too heavy, they can slide off: that's called avalanche! Avalanches are as dangerous as their reputation says. They can gain tremendous speed and power as they roar down the mountainside, hurling tons of snow into the air. Avalanches can become white tidal waves, destroying almost everything in their paths. So when you are cross-country skiing or snowshoeing it is very important to approach steep, open slopes with extreme caution. Cracks on the surface indicate unstable conditions within the snow pack. You may have experienced the collapse of a snow layer if, while standing on top of the snow, you heard a deep, "WOOMPH!" Suddenly, the platform you were standing on dropped a few inches—or even a few feet—and cracks appeared, running out beyond your ski tips like snow snakes. It is so easy to forget the secret life of snow. We need to be aware, always, of its changing, forceful personality—especially when we're out in it!

SNOW GEOLOGY

If you want to see what *pukak* looks like, you can dig a snow pit. All you need are a small shovel and some fairly deep snow. Find a level spot, then begin digging a hole about two or three feet wide, until you reach the ground. Look closely at the walls of this pit and you will be able to see the different layers of snow. This is called a snow profile, and what you are discovering is "snow geology."

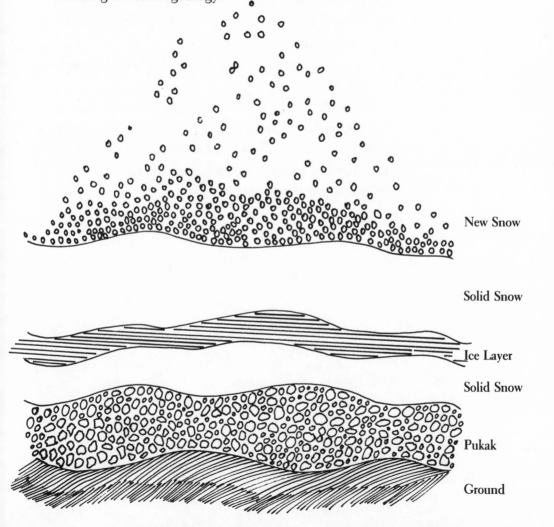

New Snow

Solid Snow

Ice Layer

Solid Snow

Pukak

Ground

Just as the Grand Canyon shows all the different layers of geologic history in rock, so your snow profile shows the winter's history. Each different layer in the snow represents a change. By learning how to read a snow profile, you can actually record storm patterns, temperature changes, and the snow's varying density. With a little practice, you can also identify different snow crystals and the kind of metamorphism that has occurred. The layer that looks like loose, sugary snow with larger air spaces between crystals is *pukak*. When viewed through a hand lens these crystals tend to be cup-shaped and larger than the others. It is not uncommon to find many layers of *pukak* within one snow profile, as they indicate warming trends between freezing periods.

Notice how much easier it is to stick your finger through *pukak* than through the more tightly compacted layers of snow above or below it. Now, run your fingertips across the band of *pukak* and imagine yourself a tiny meadow vole!

SIX

QALI
Snow That Collects
Horizontally on Trees

Qali:
A nest of snow
lies in the arms of a quaking aspen.
Young Raven mistakes it
for his home of last spring.
As the black bird lands,
his weight triggers a release.
Arched boughs bounce back
as their burden
falls free:
snow crystals
slowly drift to earth.
Chickadee dangles upside-down,
hunting
for seeds and dormant insects.
Sometimes—
if you walk
under these snow canopies,
you can hear
Earth-Spirits
calling.

Have you ever been cross-country skiing or walking through an enchanted evergreen forest when, suddenly, a branch released its burden and a clump of snow fell *plop* onto your head? If so, you have had your first introduction to *qali*—snow that collects horizontally on trees.

Qali generally forms when the air is cold and still and the sunlight diffuses through tree branches. These conditions can be found throughout the taiga regions of the world, places such as interior Siberia, Canada, Alaska, and parts of Yellowstone National Park in Wyoming. *Qali* may also occur in other sections of the Rocky Mountains.

Qali plays a key role in helping an evergreen forest change and grow, by replacing old trees with new ones. Here's how it works: As snow builds up on the boughs or branches of trees, becoming *qali*, its weight increases. Eventually, a breaking point is reached. Unless the wind blows *qali* off or the sun melts it, a weak branch will inevitably snap. In many cases, whole trees will bend and break. As this happens again and again, the canopy of boughs opens up, creating a "window" or glade in the forest. Young trees that once lived in the shadow of larger, more mature trees can now grow rapidly, responding to the additional light. Green leafy plants also begin to grow on the forest floor. They're joined by a shower of needles from broken and dying evergreen trees. The green plants and the needles together crowd out the mosses, which would otherwise suffocate young trees. Then, with the mosses gone and the sun shining through, deciduous trees begin to grow: willow, alder, birch, and aspen. These trees mature, and soon a healthy forest community of woody plants and wildflowers is flourishing.

Before too long, little evergreens begin to sprout and grow, mingling with the deciduous trees. Eventually they grow tall and crowd out the other vegetation, blocking out the sunlight once again. This is an example of what ecologists call a climax forest. Year after year, snow will fall, and *qali* will accumulate on evergreen boughs; again the branches will break, another window in the woods will appear—and the cycle of forest change will repeat itself.

Qali performs other roles in the forest ecology. For one thing, it is a roadblock to tree travel. Some pine martens and squirrels—dwellers in the spruce, fir, and pine communities—are stopped by *qali* from branch-to-branch leaping and bounding. This can make it more difficult to catch prey or escape from predators, and hinder tree dwellers from getting to their food caches. Chickadees seem to migrate to areas where aspen and birch grow high on the mountainside, avoiding the evergreen forests where *qali* accumulates heavily. Like some other birds, chickadees store seeds and insects for winter use in cracks and crevices along branches, so they need branches that are free from snow. *Qali* also forces some small birds to forage on the underside of branches, where the bark is still exposed. And *qali* bends the tender shoots of willows, alders, and birch to the ground, providing both a food supply and a warm, snug cavity in the snow for the snowshoe hare. Here, the camouflaged hare can find refuge from predators and the biting temperatures of wintery nights.

   Qali decorates the midwinter forest more beautifully

than any ornaments on a Christmas tree. The white snow resting in the arms of the evergreens creates a feeling of peace. The forest is hushed, except for the occasional crack of a breaking branch. But don't be deceived: a gentle breeze could dislodge a clump of *qali*, maybe even on you!

BUILD A "QALIMETER"

You can collect your own *qali* instead of standing around
waiting for it to fall on your head. Find some round
sticks or dowels of different diameters, and lay them
crosswise between two benches or other supports. Put
this homemade instrument in front of a window in a
place where snow can fall freely but that is sheltered
from winds. Then sit back and watch what happens.
As the snow falls—if conditions are just right for *qali*
formation—you will be able to watch it build up on
your "qalimeter." Afterward, use a ruler to measure
the amount of snow that has collected in a given time
on each stick. From your observations, do you think
that more *qali* will accumulate on a big branch or a
little branch? Why?

SEVEN

KANIK
Rime

Kanik:
Northern Lights flicker,
then fade.
Puffs of warm, moist air
tumble in, and
brush against
the cold skins of spruces—
contact,
freeze and
cover!
The evergreens look forever white
as their trunks
are veiled with ice.
Gyrfalcon cries out—
Arctic Fox jumps over blue shadows.
The snow squeaks a warning;
a tiny vole quivers
and nudges his way
deeper into the pack.
The breeze moves along,
moves on.

If you have ever reached into your freezer to pull out an ice tray and found your fingers stuck to the cold aluminum surface, you are very close to understanding the principle behind *kanik*.

Kanik, as the Kobuk Eskimos call it, or rime, the scientific name, is not snow at all. Instead, it is a vaporlike cloud or mist that freezes when it makes contact with a colder surface. In other words, the connection between your warm skin and the cold ice tray, which causes your fingers to stick, is like the connection warm air makes when it strikes a colder object—perhaps a tree—and freezes into rime.

Kanik can form on a falling snowflake, an exposed branch or tree trunk, or any other object in its path. The amount deposited may range from a light frosting to an enormous hunk of ice several feet thick, enough to snap the limbs of a substantial tree. *Kanik* has many personalities. It may look like a delicate fern frond or beautiful slender ice needles; perhaps you have seen the latter on your windowpanes. Or it may create thick, weirdly shaped projections like gargoyles on a building.

Unlike *qali*, the soft, fluffy snow that collects horizontally on trees, *kanik* forms on vertical surfaces. The warm, moving air collides with stationary objects and immediately freezes, as though a fairy had tapped her magic wand. And because *kanik* always "grows" into the prevailing wind, it's an excellent indicator of windstorm direction.

Kanik has its dangerous side. Scientists have suggested that *kanik* causes the instability of some snow layers, which may contribute to avalanches. A layer of heavily rimed crystals such as graupel—crystals coated with *kanik*—creates an icy surface off which other layers may slide. *Kanik* can also play havoc with meteorological equipment, completely covering wind sensors and other weather instruments.

Kanik is one of winter's most mysterious phenomena. It is like a wizard whose warm touch places all life under a frozen spell.

MAGIC BREATH

Have you ever awakened early in the morning to find a beautiful pattern of frozen crystals on your window-panes? This is actually another form of *kanik,* and you can imitate the way it happens. On the next very, very cold winter day, blow some of your warm breath onto a window from outside your house. What do you think will happen? Is "Jack Frost nipping at your window"— or is something else going on?

UPSIK
Wind-beaten Snow

Upsik:
Taku, the wind, has come
to sculpt the snow.
Air like a whirling knife
comes rushing in,
carving deep impressions
into the land.
Frozen dunes,
like statues of ice,
are left behind.
Wolf's paws
hardly make a dent.
He eyes the pack
and runs with vigor.
Raw days and ravenous nights
leave little room for error:
persevere or perish.

All snow forms begin as *annui*, or falling snow, and rest momentarily as *api*, or snow on the ground. Then, as the snow crystal matures, it not only changes its structure but may even be moved from one place to another. One kind of "transported" snow is called *upsik*.

Upsik is hard, wind-worked snow found in the Arctic regions of the world. Winds blow forcefully across uneven surfaces, such as mountain peaks or knolls, and sweep the top layers of snow downward. The winds then pack this displaced snow tightly into depressions or natural potholes. Sometimes these snow packs are several hundred yards deep—for instance, in gullies and stream beds. Meanwhile, on the tops of nearby hills and ridges, the short tundra vegetation remains exposed.

The firmly packed *upsik* serves as a winter highway for both animals and humans. Because it is extremely dense, *upsik* can easily support the weight of a person even without skis or snowshoes. On the wind-hardened snow of open tundra, the Eskimo sled or *kumitik*, is the perfect vehicle for transportation. It slides upon two wooden runners and is unsurpassed in its lightness and ruggedness. In the forested taiga, however, where snow tends to be very soft, fluffy, and deep, the ideal vehicle for the Eskimo is the toboggan. This is a long, light, flat-bottomed sled, made of thin boards that are curved up at the front end.

Inuits also take advantage of *upsik* by using it to build their igloos. There are times when wind compacts

the snow so tightly that even an axe cannot break it up. In such cases, a special saw is used to cut *upsik* into blocks.

Upsik can be an impenetrable barrier to grazing animals. Because they can dig through even heavy *upsik*, the mighty musk oxen are the only large herbivores that do not migrate from the tundra. Pawing vigorously with their sturdy hooves, they can obtain food from below the surface. But *upsik* does not always reach such density. Smaller animals such as the Arctic fox, varying hare, and ptarmigan can usually find areas with less dense snow, where they can dig in and cover themselves.

Where the wind howls with the wolves, *upsik* can be found. It is steel snow!

SIQOQ
Swirling or Drifting Snow

Siqoq:
High on the ridge
new snow is dancing;
call it a swirling snowstorm.
Snow plumes rise
higher and higher
until they curl under,
as wind tosses surface crystals
this way and that.
Down in the valley,
Eskimo and Wolf
hide behind
screens of smoky snow,
pursuing Caribou.
Each one
remembers mysteries
that accompany them
in the stalk.

If you were to go outside on a crisp day in January and look up along a mountain ridge, you might see what look like puffs of smoke encircling the peaks. The Inuits of the Kobuk Valley use the word *siqoq* to describe these fine snow particles blown upward by the wind. *Siqoq*, or swirling snow, is created when winds rise from the valley floor in a circling or spiraling motion that blows snow from the tops of exposed drifts. Sometimes, as the wind's speed increases, the snowy veil rises higher and higher, becoming a screen of dancing snow crystals.

Siqoq can produce spectacular white-outs, in which it is easy for travelers to get lost. You can get some idea of what these white-outs are like by looking at a popular toy—the winter scene enclosed in a small plastic dome filled with water. As your hand shakes the dome, an intense flurry of white snowflakes clouds your view of the tranquil setting. Seconds later, as the hand (the wind in real life) quiets down, the small flakes return to the bottom of the dome.

There are really two kinds of *siqoq*: swirling snow,

which we've just been talking about, and drifting snow. Drifting snow, the gentler version of *siqoq*, helps determine the growth patterns of plants. Plants that need insulation from the cold tend to grow on the sheltered side of a slope, where *siqoq* forms deep drifts. Deeper snow offers more protection. Hardier plants, on the other hand, can remain exposed on the windy side.

Swirling snow, the fiercer form of *siqoq*, launches ice crystals as hard as bones at the small branches and needles of evergreens, until they're worn away. Such conditions can create a low, gnarled form of tree growth known as krummholz. These contorted trees, sculpted by the elements, look something like frozen dwarfs in a white desert. They can usually be seen on high exposed ridges, near the upper limits of where trees can grow.

Animals have adapted to *siqoq* in various ways. Musk oxen have a particularly clever adaptation: they mark their trails on sparse woody vegetation by rubbing their forefeet on special scent glands located beneath their eyes. In this way they leave behind a scent trail they can follow easily in case the swirling *siqoq* is too dense for them to see.

Ptarmigan and varying hares use both kinds of *siqoq*. When swirling *siqoq* creates a white-out, they often seek shelter and food in the cavities and depressions formed by drifting *siqoq*. Wolves and arctic people use *siqoq* too—as a moving screen to hide behind while stalking caribou.

Siqoq, snow blown upward by the wind, can be a swirling dancer high above the ridge, or drifting snow that rolls across the land like foamy surf. Either way, *siqoq* is always on the move!

SOME LIKE IT DEEP

During the summer, look at a mountainside and try
to guess what type of snow cover used to be there.
Deep? Shallow? Was the slope exposed, or covered
heavily with drifted *siqoq?*

The kind of plant growth we see in summer can tell
us how deep the snow was in winter. Where you find
sagebrush, bitterbrush, and scrub oak, snow depths
were probably shallow. But if you see chokecherries,
quaking aspens, or evergreens, chances are the snow
was much deeper. If you look closely you may even
see different types of vegetation on different sides of
the same mountain. Why do you think that is?

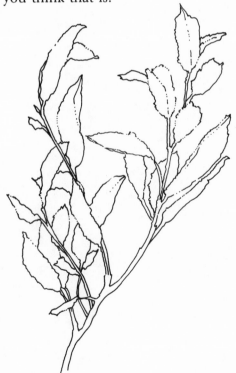

KIMOAGRUK
Snow Drift

Kimoagruk:
Only a few hours of daylight remain—
a man and a woman are caught
in the start of a blizzard.
Time is not with them.
Looking back,
their tracks have
vanished. Ahead,
no home in sight.
But winter has made hostels
for snow travelers.
Where the wind races, then drops,
usually at the crest of a hill,
a drift develops.
To anxious wanderers,
it is a refuge.
They dig out the snow in whispers
and say,
"Keep me safe."

If you have ever frosted a cake, you'll remember the artistic swirls you can make as you glide the frosting across the baked surface. With each lift of the knife, you create an upward curl where a greater amount of frosting is deposited. In your mind now, if you substitute *siqoq* (swirling snow) for frosting, the upward curls or overhangs become snowdrifts—*kimoagruk*, as the Kobuk people call them.

Kimoagruk, then, is basically *siqoq* piled up and at rest. To the Inuit people of Canada these drifts are also known as *barkans* or *kalatoqoniq*. As the tiny particles of *siqoq* become exposed to the windy side of the mountain, they are forced downhill. When the wind gusts strongly, then stops, they bond together in a process known as sintering and form compacted snow drifts—*kimoagruk*.

In a more advanced stage of *kimoagruk*, the wind may erode or carve away the base of the drift more rapidly than the top surface, making the drift look like a white anvil. These overhanging drifts are called *mapsuk*.

If the wind carving is really extreme, the *kimoagruk* may end up looking like an eerie piece of ice sculpture. This snow sculpturing is called *zastraq* by the Russians, *skavler* by the Norwegians, and *kaioqlaq* by the Inuits of Canada. The snow mass eventually may be worn away completely, until the snow crystals are freed to regroup as *siqoq*. Then the cycle beings all over again.

In winter, large snowdrifts may completely fill gullies; come spring, they melt and become reservoirs, providing water for plants and animals throughout the short Arctic summer. Some *kimoagruks* last well into June or July, serving as an oasis of water in an otherwise barren environment. The environments of Arctic and alpine (high mountain) areas are in many ways like that of a desert; the main characteristic of each is dry-

ness. Because high winds dry out soil and plants, Arctic and alpine vegetation grows close to the ground, looking much like tiny mats or pin cushions. These plants have long root systems that act as anchors to secure them against the wind, and also as straws to draw out moisture from the parched soil.

A very large *kimoagruk* may not melt until late in the summer. Drifts of this kind are known as *zaboi* by the Russians. In extreme cases, they may slow down the growth of plants or even stop them from growing at all!

In some places, wind currents scoop out the snow around a *kimoagruk*, forming cavities known as *arja-marja*. Because the vegetation is uncovered, it is easily available to animals, so these are wonderful places to observe wildlife.

Along with offering special aid to plants and wildlife, a *kimoagruk* can also provide protection for people. Many a weary wanderer, suffering from biting Arctic temperatures, has sought refuge inside a hollowed-out snowdrift. Snuggled safely inside the *kimoagruk*, a person can usually find temperatures ten to twenty degrees warmer than on the "outside."

Large drifts also may be excellent indicators as to where *not* to build highways or railroads. If we could learn to read snow landscapes more closely, we'd have fewer highways with hazardous ice buildup or dangerous wind conditions.

As snow falls and blows and falls some more, it is comforting to know that *kimoagruk* can be a home away from home.

INUIT SNOW SHELTER

For the Kobuk Eskimos, who live in a relatively flat, forested environment, really big snowdrifts are not easy to find. So the Kobuk people create their own snow shelters by piling up loose snow in a big, circular heap, using a snowshoe to help shovel. Later, after the snow crystals have settled and bonded together, the Kobuks return to dig out comfortable living quarters inside. The Kobuk people call this snow shelter a *quin-zhee*. *Quin-zhees* offer considerable warmth and protection from the elements. Often, an individual *quin-zhee* will be used repeatedly, because it can serve as an emergency resting place between trap lines and home.

You could try building your own *quin-zhee!* (It goes faster if you have friends to help you.) First, stomp out a large circle in the snow about ten feet in diameter, to outline the place where your *quin-zhee* will be. Next, make a big pile of snow about six to eight feet high within your circle. (A shovel makes this easier.) Then go away for about two hours, so that the snow will have plenty of time to settle and compact. When you come back, you can begin to dig out an entrance. It should be fairly small to keep the cold air out, but large enough so you can get in—usually about two feet high and wide. Once inside you can hollow out the interior, throwing the snow out through the entrance. It's a lot like carving out a pumpkin! Finally, carve yourself a bench in the snow walls and light a candle. Can you imagine yourself sheltering here from an Arctic blizzard?

ELEVEN

QAMANIQ
Bowl-shaped Hollow
Around the Base of a Tree

Qamaniq:
Snow falls freely
on Forest's floor,
except when evergreens
snatch earthbound flakes.
The snow held by trees
creates a space below;
shallow snow.
You will find no animals here—
this is a hushed hollow.
Death may sting prematurely.
Better to wait
with the turning constellations
for Spring's warming hand.
It touches bitter snow shadows,
turning them into
islands of life;
Birds, Mammals, Insects, and Plants
appear and
congregate.

Have you ever taken refuge from a snowstorm under a spruce, fir, or pine tree? If not, you should try it, for the thickly needled boughs act like arms to catch falling snowflakes, preventing most of them from landing on you.

As the branches collect earthbound flakes, snow depth becomes unequal on the forest floor. Where there are no trees, the crystals fall freely, adding inches to the blanket of snow stretched across the meadow or glade. But where evergreens stand guard, their branches intercept much of the snow. The small amount that does reach the ground quickly melts and evaporates, leaving a hollow or "snow shadow" beneath the trees. This bowl-shaped well found around the base of evergreens is called *qamaniq* by the Kobuk.

Small mammals avoid *qamaniq* during the colder months of winter, for the shallow snow offers little insulating warmth or protection from predators. Sometimes though, as we learned earlier, heavy *qali* formations build up along the pine boughs and weigh them down; if the branches bend far enough towards the ground, they create cozy cubbyholes within the *qamaniq*. These caverns make an excellent night refuge for snowshoe hares and other animals.

As winter fades and temperatures begin to rise, the once inhospitable *qamaniq* becomes an island of spring. Grouse, juncos, and white-crowned sparrows gather here with other migratory birds in search of food. They know that inside the *qamaniq* insects are moving about, seeds and plants are coming to life—all creating a bustling little community in the midst of an otherwise still and hostile environment. Nearby meadows are still covered by their cold winter quilt, while these snow shadows become completely free of snow, providing the first glimpses of early flowers such as spring beauties, dog-toothed violets, and marsh marigolds.

On a warm day in mid-March or April, look into a *qamaniq*. You may find steam rising from the black, matted soil. Tiny sprigs of vegetation are uncurling. It's the first touch of sun the earth has felt for a long, long time!

TWELVE

SIQOQTOAQ
Sun Crust

Siqoqtoaq:
Spring is loosening
Winter's grip.
Melting days and freezing nights
turn the snowpack
into sun crust.
Snowy Owl lands a lemming.
Change blows warmly through.
The sky wears royal blue.
Birds wing their way back north
to nest in Tundra's cradle.
Grizzly sniffs the air.
Thaw!
Color comes back to the country
as springs of vegetation unfurl.
The Kobuk people journey south,
carrying songs for their children.

When the groundhog's shadow becomes a permanent fixture on the snow, *siqoqtoaq*, or sun crust, is probably being made. As daytime temperatures begin to rise, the snow crystals expand, becoming wet and granular.(Skiers know this as "corn snow" or spring slush.) When the sun sets, temperatures often drop well below freezing again, and the melting, sunkissed snow hardens into an icy layer like a sheet of frosted glass. On a crisp moonlit evening, this "glass" can even reflect stars. Thousands of snow crystals shimmer under the full moon, throwing out colors like tiny prisms. The snow will even carry you as you walk across it!

This frozen condition is also known as *nast*, a Russian word meaning "a thickened crust on the surface of a mature snow cover."

When the nights are relatively warm, melting water percolating down through the *siqoqtoaq* can cause heavy, wet snowslides. When nights are cold and days are warm, however, the snowpack is stabilized and becomes ideal for spring skiing.

Visible changes also take place on the surface of

siqoqtoaq. In high altitudes and latitudes, springtime brings ever-longer periods of intense sunlight while the air temperature remains far below freezing. The moisture in the air crystallizes on the cold surface of the snow, like frozen dew. This can transform the surface snowflakes into long, vertical needles called *qulu*. A snowfield covered with *qulu* looks like the raised hackles of an irritated wolf.

While the *siqoqtoaq* is frozen, large animals such as elk and moose can use it as a highway. At this time of year they are migrating out of the river bottoms and valleys to the high country, reversing the journey they make each autumn. Sometimes, however, *siqoqtoaq* can become extremely troublesome. Sharp edges that develop in cracks or break-throughs in the icy layer become sharp as razors, quick to slice flesh or wound

paws or hooves, leaving an animal vulnerable to a
watching predator.

In the Arctic, both wolves and Inuits use this time
of *siqoqtoaq* to their advantage. They will follow a
caribou herd along the sun crust, waiting until one of
the animals breaks through. As the distressed caribou

flounders, it becomes easy prey for the lighter wolf or Kobuk hunter. The destruction of large numbers of animals—even an entire species in a certain area—can be caused by these treacherous icy crusts. But sometimes this is necessary to prevent an animal population from growing too large for its food supply. Nature keeps things in balance.

Siqoqtoaq in its frozen aspect may also make it difficult for smaller animals, such as voles or shrews, to reach the protective space between snow and ground. If they venture to the surface while the crust has melted and remain outside too long, they may find their way back frozen shut. A hungry fox will eat them for dinner, if the icy cold doesn't get them first.

There is also a more colorful side to *siqoqtoaq*. In late spring or early summer, patches of pink or red snow appear in the *siqoqtoaq*. If you kneel down next to this colored snow, you will find yourself immediately under its spell, for it bears the wonderful aroma of watermelon. In fact, it is nicknamed "watermelon snow." But it isn't watermelon, at all—not this far north! The color and smell are actually caused by a kind of algae that finds *siqoqtoaq* ideal for its existence. But don't give in to the temptation of a watermelon-flavored sno-cone—it will really upset your stomach!

Plants that grow in Arctic or alpine conditions are extremely hardy. They must be, in order to survive. Hardiest of all are a few species that grow and blossom in the very short time between the end of winter, when

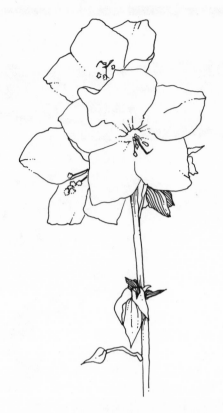

the snow melts, and the beginning of summer, when most species start to flourish. They are called *spring ephemerals*, which literally means, "lasting only a very short time." These small, tenacious plants occupy a special niche in the cycle of seasons, drawing on resources of light, water, and nutrients that will be used by larger species later in the summer.

One spring ephemeral is the alpine buttercup. It grows at high elevations, where it is exposed to drastic changes in climate, ranging from sudden and violent storms to periods of extreme drought. The growing season is short; temperatures frequently fall below freezing at night; and winds and frost reduce available soil moisture. This plant must mature quickly in order to complete its full growth cycle: it will emerge, grow, blossom, and set seed all in a matter of weeks. As if by magic, the buttercups spring up and bloom almost as soon as the snow melts. They can be found growing under the edges of snowdrifts, sometimes pushing up through two to three inches of snow and ice. The heat a growing plant gives off is enough to melt a hole in the snow about an inch or so in diameter!

Special adaptations enable arctic plants to triumph over incredibly difficult conditions. The flowering parts of the spring beauty are fully formed while still under snow cover. Other tundra plants are even more persistent, producing not seeds, but baby plants, to help ensure their tenuous survival. Masses of fireweed in full bloom have been found frozen stiff, but the following day, after thawing, they showed no evidence of frost damage as their bright pink flowers waved against the blue sky!

Spring in snow country is a passionate time. Winter's blanket is turned down as the sun burns away the last snow crystals. The uncovered ground is bare and moist, matted by January's thumb. Within days, little cushions of green grasses and mosses push their heads up through brown litter, followed by an array of early bloomers. It is said that wildflowers can signal the coming events in the natural world. When dog-toothed violets or glacier lilies begin to flower, listen for the mating calls of the saw-whet owl and be careful where you walk—the mule deer

is bedding down to give birth to her fawns. Yellow fritillary, one of the earliest flowers of spring, fortells the return of meadowlarks, the courtship displays of sage grouse, and the nest-building of Canada geese.

The transformation is rapid. Each day brings cause for celebration, for as the snow creeps back, new life bursts forth. In the aspen groves, mountain bluebirds and ruby-crowned kinglets begin their courtship rituals, while in the high meadows, elk calves are being dropped in the soft grass and coyote pups are learning how to entertain the night with their high-pitched howls.

To the people of the Kobuk Valley, *siqoqtoaq* is gone. The Arctic is in bloom. Rhododendrons rise like fuch-

sia trumpets, heralding the arrival of spring. Endless
daylight transforms the rhythms of the Far North, and
the rebirth of life is sudden and vibrant. Thousands
upon thousands of migrating birds return to the tundra
to nest. Feathers blow across the landscape, a reminder
of past snow flurries. The people turn their backs to
the fading northern lights and feel the approach of the
midnight sun. The Kobuk River, swollen with snow
language, carries winter away.

An old Eskimo woman once said:

"The snow that greets us, stays with us, goes away crying. I watch the snow cry. My grandson says it is melting. I say no, it is crying. Who likes to leave?"

HIBERNATING PLANTS

The ability of some plants to develop beneath snow cover is a fascinating phenomenon. Perhaps you have gathered wildflower seeds in late summer and early fall, and saved them for next spring's garden, only to find that they never sprouted. This is because wildflowers and most native plants need to have a period of dormancy, or rest; winter's freezing temperatures place them in a kind of suspended animation. In a sense, they undergo a deep sleep much like hibernating animals. As the soil loosens during the spring thaw, light filters down through layers of snow and the spark of life within these plants is ignited.

If you wish to propagate wildflowers of any kind, you need to recreate as accurately as possible the environmental conditions they experience in the wild. Let your seeds "hibernate" in a freezer until mid-February or March, and you may get amazing results when you plant them in April or May.

What's in a Name?

We have been talking about some of the names for different kinds of snow in the Kobuk Eskimo language. We have also used the names of many plants and animals that live in the Far North. But these plants and animals have other names—names that all scientists understand even if they don't speak English.

In 1735 a Swedish naturalist named Carl Linnaeus developed a universal system of classification for all living things. He realized that the growing body of knowledge about plants and animals needed a method of organization in order to avoid confusion, since the common name of an organism generally varies from one country to another.

For example, here are different common names for the bird we in America call the English sparrow:

House sparrow (*England*)   Passera oltramontana (*Italy*)
Moineau domestique (*France*) Haussperling (*Germany*)
Gorrion (*Spain*)   Musch (*Holland*)
Pardal (*Portugal*)   Graaspurv (*Denmark*
Hussparf (*Sweden*)   and Norway*)

You can begin to see how confusing this business of naming living things really is!

So Linnaeus came up with a naming system that we call *binomial nomenclature*. In this system, each living thing is designated by a *genus* (the first name) and *species* (the second name). These two-part names are all Latin. Why? Because if we look back into history, until the eighteenth century most books were written in Latin, the language of scholars. Most of the general population could not read. But, as printed books began appearing in other countries, written in their native languages, the use of Latin was retained for technical descriptions and names of plants and animals.

By using Linnaeus's binomial nomenclature, or scientific language, a biologist in the United States can communicate with a biologist in Russia. They both know that *Passer domesticus* means "English sparrow" to any biologist, anywhere in the world.

Here is a list of the plants, birds, and mammals discussed in this book. See if you can become familiar with their scientific (Latin) names. They're not as hard to pronounce as they look—try saying one syllable at a time.

One more note: You will see that the abbreviation *sp.* is used in some of the scientific names. This stands for *species*, as in *Betula sp.* (birch species). It means that there are several types of birches in the *Betula* genus, or group. For example, if your name were Smith, you and your brothers and sisters would be *Smith sp.*

Common and Scientific Names of Plants, Birds, and Mammals Mentioned in this Book

PLANTS

Common Name	Scientific Name
Alder	*Alnus sp.*
Alpine buttercup	*Ranunculus adoneus*
Birch	*Betula sp.*
Blue-green algae	*Phylum cyanophyta*
Cloudberry (Western thimbleberry)	*Rubus parriflorus*
Cottongrass (cotton-sedge)	*Eriophorum augustifolium*
Dog-toothed violet	*Erythronium grandiflorum*
Fireweed	*Epilobium latifolium*
Glacier lily	*Erythronium grandiflorum*
Poplar	*Populus sp.*
Reindeer lichen	*Cladonia rangiferina*
Rhododendron	*Rhododendron sp.*
Spring beauty	*Claytonia lanceolata*
Black spruce	*Picea mariana*
White spruce	*Picea glauca*
Yellow fritillary	*Fritillaria pudica*
Willow	*Salix sp.*

BIRDS

Mountain bluebird	*Sialia currucoides*
Black-capped chickadee	*Parus atricapillus*
Mountain chickadee	*Parus gambeli*
Bald eagle	*Haliaeetus leucocephalus*
Common eider	*Somateria mollissima*
Cassin's finch	*Carpodacus cassinii*
Canada goose	*Branta canadensis*
Blue grouse	*Dendragapus obscurus*

Common Name	Scientific Name
Sage grouse	*Centrocercus urophasianus*
Gyrfalcon	*Falco rusticolus*
Rough-legged hawk	*Buteo lagopus*
Oregon junco	*Junco oregonus*
Ruby-crowned kinglet	*Regulus calendula*
Arctic loon	*Gavia arctica*
Common loon	*Gavia immer*
Western meadowlark	*Sturnella neglecta*
Clark's nutcracker	*Nucifraga columbiana*
Great gray owl	*Strix nebulosa*
Great horned owl	*Bubo virginianus*
Saw-whet owl	*Aegolius acadicus*
Snowy owl	*Nyctea scandiaca*
Willow ptarmigan	*Lagopus lagopus*
California quail	*Callipepla californica*
Common raven	*Corvus corax*
White-crowned sparrow	*Zonotrichia leucophyrs*

MAMMALS

Little brown bat	*Myotis lucifugus*
Black bear	*Euarctos americanus*
Brown bear	*Ursusarctos middendorffi*
Grizzly bear	*Ursusarctos horribilis*
Polar bear	*Thalarctos maritimus*
Beaver	*Castor canadensis*
Bison	*Bison bison*
Caribou	*Rangifer sp.*
Domestic cat	*Felis domesticus*
Least chipmunk	*Eutamias minimus*
Coyote	*Canis latrans*
Mule deer	*Odocoileus hemionus*
Dolphin	*Delphinus sp.*

Common Name	Scientific Name
North American Elk	*Cervus canadensis*
Arctic fox	*Alopex lagopus*
Snowshoe hare	*Lepus americanus*
Varying hare	*Lepus timidus*
Varying lemming	*Lemmus sp.*
Canadian Lynx	*Lynx canadensis*
Woolly mammoth*	*Mammuthus primigenius*
Marmot	*Marmota flaviventris*
Pine marten	*Martes americana*
Moose	*Alces alces*
Deer mouse	*Peromyscus maniculatus*
Jumping mouse	*Zapus sp.*
Musk oxen	*Ovibos moschatus*
Pika	*Ochotona princeps*
Pig	*Sus scrofa*
Porcupine	*Erethizon dorsatum*
Prairie dog	*Cynomys sp.*
Pronghorn	*Antilocapra americana*
Raccoon	*Procyon lotor*
Woolly rhinocerus*	*Coelodonta sp.*
Alaskan fur seal	*Callorhinus ursinus*
Bighorn sheep	*Ovis canadensis*
Dall sheep	*Ovis dalli*
Masked shrew	*Sorex cinereus*
Striped skunk	*Mephitis mephitis*
Ground squirrel	*Citellus sp.*
Red squirrel	*Tamiasciurus hudsonicus*
Meadow vole	*Microtus pennsylvanicus*
Long-tailed weasel	*Mustela frenata*
Humpback whale	*Megaptera novaeangliae*
Timber wolf	*Canis lupus*
Walrus	*Odobenus rosmarus*
Wolverine	*Gulo luscus*

*extinct

Bibliography

Billings, W. D., and Bliss, L. C. "An Alpine Snowbank Environment and Its Effect on Vegetation: Plan and Development and Productivity." *Ecology*, Vol. 40, No. 3.

Bliss, L. C. "Adaptations of Arctic and Alpine Plants to Environmental Conditions." *AAAS Symposium: Life Under Extreme Conditions*, New York City, December 1960.

Boaz, Franz. "The Central Eskimo," Sixth Annual Report of Bureau of Ethnology, 1888.

————"Eskimo Tales." *Journal of American Folklore*, Vol. 7, 1894.

————"Folklore of the Eskimo." *Journal of American Folklore*, Vol. 17, 1904.

Craighead, John, J.; Craighead, Frank C., Jr.; and Davis, Ray J. *A Field Guide to Rocky Mountain Wildflowers*. Boston: Houghton Mifflin, 1963.

Culin, Stewart. *Games of the North American Indians*. New York: Dover, 1975.

Formozov, A. N. "On the Significance of the Structure of the Snow Cover in the Ecology and Geography of Mammals and Birds." In Aka. Nauk, USSR, 1961. "Snow Cover as an Integral Factor of the Environment and Its Importance in the Ecology of Mammals and Birds." Materials for Fauna, Flora of the U.S.S.R. New Series, Zoology, 5 (xx) 1946:1–15Z. Translation by William Prychodko and William O. Pruitt. Published by Boreal Institute for Northern Studies, University of Alberta, Occasional Publication No. 1, 1964.

Giddings, J. L. *Kobuk River People*. Fairbanks: University of Alaska, 1961.

Hamilton, W. J. "Winter Sleep." *Audubon Nature Bulletin*.

Hanson, Herbert C. "Vegetation Types in Northwestern Alaska: Comparisons with Communities in other Arctic Regions." *Ecology*, Vol. 34, No. 1, January 1953.

Irving, Laurence. "Adaptations to Cold." *Scientific American*, Vol. 214, No. 1, January 1966, pp. 94–101.

Kimball, Steven L., and Salisbury, Frank. "Plant Development Under Snow." *Botanical Gazette* 135:147–149, 1974.

Kirk, Ruth. *Snow*. New York: Morrow, 1977.

Kroeber. "Animal Tales of the Eskimo." *Journal of American Folklore*. Vol. 12, 1899.

LaChapelle, Edward. *Field Guide to Snow Crystals*. Seattle: University of Washington Press, 1969.

Lowenstein, Tom. *Eskimo Poems from Canada and Greenland*. University of Pittsburgh Press, 1973.

Major, Ted. *Snow Ecology*. Boulder, Colorado: Thorne Ecological Institute, 1979.

Miller, Albert, *Meteorology*, Columbus, Ohio: Merrill Publishing Co., 1971.

Mohr, Charles. "The Ways of Wildlife in Winter." *Audubon Nature Bulletin*, 1961.

Perla, Ronald I. and M. Mortinelli *Avalanche Handbook* U.S. Dept. of Agriculture; Agriculture Handbook #489, 1976.

Pruitt, William O. *Animals of the North*. New York: Harper & Row, 1967.

———"Animals in the Snow." *Scientific American* No. 202, 1960.

———*Boreal Ecology*. London: Edward Arnold, 1978.

———"Snow as a Factor in the Winter Ecology of Barren Ground Caribou." *Arctic*, Vol. 12, No. 3, 1959.

Spencer, Robert F. *The North Alaska Eskimo: A Study in Ecology and Society*. Bureau of American Ethnology, Bulletin 171, 1959.

Stokes, Donald W. *A Guide to Nature in Winter*. Boston: Little, Brown & Co., 1976.

Tener, J.S., *Muskoxen*, Ottawa, Canada: Queen's Printer and Controller of Stationery, 1965. Department of Northern Affairs and National Resources, Canadian Wildlife Service.

Index

Italicized numbers indicate illustrations.

Terry Tempest Williams is a freelance writer specializing in the natural world and native North American cultures. She received a B.S. in English and an M.S. in Environmental Education from the University of Utah, and in 1977 was the recipient of the Murie-Broome Book Award given by the Wilderness Society for achievement in natural history or conservation subjects. She currently is Associate Curator at the Utah Museum of Natural History. *The Secret Language of Snow* is her first book.

Ted Major is a naturalist and a leading teacher of winter ecology. He holds a B.S. in Animal Husbandry from Utah State University and an M.S. in Science Education from the University of Utah. He also did postgraduate work at Cornell University in botany. He is founder and Director Emeritus of the Teton Science School. The Thorne Ecological Institute in Boulder, Colorado, where he was a consultant, published his book *Snow Ecology*. Mr. Major is currently cross-country ski operations manager at Yellowstone National Park.

Jennifer Dewey has illustrated several books for children and adults, including *Living Fossils* and *Song of the Sea Otter*. Specializing in the art of the natural world, Ms. Dewey also illustrates posters for public interest groups and the National Park Service. She studied at the Rhode Island School of Design and now lives in Santa Fe, New Mexico.